SOCIAL MEDIA MARKETING TIPS

I0393524

BEST MEDIA MARKETING STRATEGIES TO MARKETING SUCCESS

By Paul D. Kings

Copyrights 2017 **Paul D. Kings**

http://www.pauldkings.com

Subscribe to my newsletter to get free information
and free books on

making money online.

Paul D. Kings

Table of Contents

Paul D. Kings

PREFACE

With the current trend in marketing, social media is now the premiere player in the success of every online business. There is no way that you will have the success you desire if you are not going to dive in and take part in the use of the developing social media melee.

As such, you should have a flexible social media marketing strategy that will work for this new and dynamic environment. Through a well-planned Search Engine Optimization marketing strategy, as illustrated in this book, you can take advantage of the social media marketing craze for your business's success. Through a great SEO marketing strategy, your website will get the links and traffic that it needs to stay up in the search engine rankings and drive sales to your business.

Social media marketing strategy, based on social networks and networking sites, is perhaps one of the most important tool for any internet marketer. The reason only very few marketing strategies have been able to prove themselves more effective than social network marketing is that social media provides a large number of potential known and unknown customers which is helpful for marketers.

The other reason that social media can be so successful is that it takes advantage of social proofing. When a customer sees that a certain business has lots of likes/followers/connections, they tend toward having trust and confidence in the business. This is similar to seeing two restaurants, one very empty and the other very busy, which one would you rather go to?

Which one do you inherently think is better than the other? You would naturally assume that the busy restaurant has better food, service, and other amenities because there are more customers there filling the place. This is what social media does for a business, it plays on the natural psychology of social proofing and allows even small businesses a large edge.

Social media marketing strategy is a better way of connecting with your customers and their circle of friends' and allows them to be added to your contact list.With the guides provided in this book, you will have an edge over the average business owner in how to empower your social media marketing strategy. You will learn many layers of internet marketing strategies to build your business as a successful internet marketer.

You will have to make several choices about your business and to apply those decisions to your business in a consistent, thoughtful, and strategic way. It will not be enough to glean one idea from this book. You will need to write down the decisions you come to along the way and make that your master to-do list. Some of these things you may already be doing, but if you tweak the other elements around those strategies, you will be more successful. I will begin from a basic standpoint and build from there.

Paul D. Kings

CHAPTER 1-WHAT IS A MEDIA STRATEGY?

A media strategy is a plan of action that helps businesses reach their target customer. By reaching out to their target customer, they strive to improve their overall conversion rate of that potential customer to a paying customer to a loyal, repeating customer. When trying to capture the attention of a niche market, it's important to know the exact demographic and what will get their attention in the most effective way.

Key Components to Consider When Creating Your Media Strategy:

Identify Your Target Market

The demographics of your target customer should be taken into consideration. If you have a car wash business, your target would be a certain geographic area around your car wash. It is a little more complicated in the online sales community. If you have an online business, your target customer would be anyone with a credit card and an internet connection. So, as you can see the more you know about your target market the more effective your overall marketing strategy will be.

You will need to identify your type of customer, where and how they spend their time, and how the customer can most effectively be reached. For example, marketing through mobile apps such as Whatsapp or game apps or Youtube commercials and social media would be more effective for reaching the teenage demographic than print and traditional media would be.

For your Baby Boomer demographic, social media is a burgeoning field as they are late adopters to the social media platforms. If you have a product or service that is specific to them, such as a hair product, targeted Facebook spots would be particularly effective. This demographic tend to like high context, trust connected products. So seeing your product there above the pictures of their grandkids and friends lends a trust component to your product that can't be replicated in any other medium

Importance of Measurable Objectives

One thing to keep in mind during the strategy process is your overall marketing objectives and goals and how you will know when you have achieved them. Your marketing goals need to be measurable and specific, both in the goal expectation and in the time you want to accomplish it. If a goal is simply, "make more money," it can be measured because more is more than you have, but there are no specifics tactics involved and you don't know when you have achieved your goal.

To borrow the SMART criteria from Peter Drucker's <u>Management by Objectives</u>, make sure your goals are clear and reachable, each one should be:

- Specific (simple, sensible, significant).
- Measurable (meaningful, motivating).
- Achievable (agreed, attainable).
- Relevant (reasonable, realistic and resourced, results-based).
- Time bound (time-based, time limited, time/cost limited, timely, time-sensitive).

"Increase profits From Amount today by 20% by x Date, Quarter 3" is a much more specific, realistic goal -- and it introduces a time aspect that creates a sense of the ability to measure and draft a workable timeline.

Determine Your Marketing Budget

In your media strategy, you must also consider your marketing budget, which involves time AND money. Without a budget, it is possible to throw tens of thousands of dollars or hundreds of hours at a problem without seeing a clear solution. However, having a set budget encourages you to think each tactic through and be more creative in your problem-solving and protects you from overspending money or time that you do not have.

The second concern is the time budget you have. At the end of the day, each customer you create has a lifetime-worth to your business. You will have to calculate what that worth is and what your time is worth.

It would not be a smart strategy spending more time resources to get a customer than they provide in lifetime-business to your business. You would have to tweak your marketing to be more efficient. Your time Return on Investment is just as important as your monetary one.

Learn From Your Results

The most effective media strategies are those that evolve over time, becoming more efficient in the time, money, and other resources they require. If you launch one strategy that doesn't produce your desired results, you can learn from where it went wrong and improve subsequent launches. This is why measuring results are important. They provide valuable data that can be implemented into future media strategies to improve them.

Because SMART goals have measurable components to them, then there are many ways to improve on each one. You could improve by increasing your sales by a larger percent or do it sooner than you had set up in your goal. You can create contests among your employees with certain benchmarks to achieve and take advantage of their natural drive to be praised and recognized with peer pressure and competition.

As long as it stays friendly, it can build your team and your sales. Involving your employees also takes advantage of their built in social media accounts, which can broaden your reach. All of their friends and family will want them to win the competition, so they will help spread the word with every like/follow/connection to boost their family or friends' standing in the competition.

Purpose of a Media Strategy

The purpose of a media strategy is entirely dependent on what your business hopes to achieve with it. Improving public relations is a completely different goal than increasing profits, but both can be achieved through a well-written, well-planned-out media strategy.

Some examples of media strategies are: rolling out a new product or service, repositioning your established brand to expand, showing your charitable giving side to your business, form stronger relationships with affiliates or referral sources, monitor your competition, or change consumer perception of the product or brand.

Different Types of Media Strategies

All media strategies take the same approach during creation. They must all have specific goals and a specific demographic n mind; however, their objectives may be totally different. In this sense, there are different types of media strategies. For example, a strategy implemented to raise awareness of a certain issue or condition is far different than a strategy than one which is used to promote the upcoming release of a product or service.

Implementation of Your Media Strategy

Who is your target customer? First thing is first. Who are you trying to reach with your message? This is important to the success of your media strategy. This step identifies where your message needs to be to hit your target customer, without this the rest of the steps have no value.

If you reach a customer who doesn't need your product or service, you won't make very many sales. What's the goal of your marketing? Be specific, this the benchmark you will use when it comes to the success of your media strategy.

What's your value proposition? Identify your value proposition or theme. What's the problem that you solve or need you fulfill and how do you go about it? That's the core or basis of your proposition and/or theme.

Set your objectives, again using the SMART method.

Research. If you struggle with any of the above, spend time doing your research with your goals and objectives in mind.

Create a prospect profile. What needs to be communicated to your customer? What's the message that will grab your target customer's attention?

Draft your message. Based on the information above you are ready to draft your message. You can use different messages, but they must all have the same objective. Don't forget to give your customer a strong call-to-action, or next action step, whether that be the use of one of your coupons or going in to see a presentation at your business or participating in your charity run or being a sponsor for your upcoming event.

Give them a way to interact with you so that you know they got the message that you sent out. You will determine your marketing results by how much participation you received from the campaign.

CHAPTER 2-HOW TO DEVELOP AN EFFECTIVE SOCIAL MEDIA MARKETING STRATEGY

Social Media Marketing Plan

Starting at the ground floor and building up, here is my overview of how to create a social media marketing plan from scratch. You may have done some of this, so evaluate yourself like it is a check list.

I like to think of this like planning a roadtrip. Start out by pointing yourself in the right direction, then choose the way you're going to get there, check in regularly to make sure you're on track, and have some fun along the way.

Step 1: Audit Your Current Social Media Marketing Presence

"Know thyself. Know the customer. Innovate." – Beth Comstock

Before you strategizes about where you are headed, take a quick look at where you are. Few areas to consider when auditing your business's social media presence are:

• Which networks are you currently active on?

• Are your networks optimized?

- This is your business' photo and cover images, bio, URL, videos, slides, infographics or GIFs etc.

- Which networks are currently bringing you the most value, in terms of conversion to customers or brand recognition?

- This is your business to customer interaction: likes, shares, comments, followers and retweets.

- Are you posting at the proper time of the day for your customer?

This would be if you are targeting students and you are posting during the day when they are likely in class, or targeting Moms and are posting during dinner time.

- What are your top social posts so you can set them up to automatically repost at a certain interval?

This would be content driven or brand driven posts, not time sensitive event posts unless you are very careful not to post them past a certain date.

- What are your leads and revenues that you are generating?

- How do your profiles compare to your competitors' profiles?

Step 2: Discover and Document Who Your Ideal Customer Is

"The aim of marketing is to know and understand the customer so well the product or service fits him and sells itself." – Peter Drucker

You will want to get as specific as possible with this part. For example, if you identified your target market as parents it would be ok. However, if you identify your ideal customer as a parent that lives in the United States, is between 30 and 50 years of age, earns over $70,000, primarily uses Facebook and has an interest in outdoors activities you will have more success crafting a campaign to appeal to this ideal customer.

Even the best marketing strategy will fail if you are marketing to the wrong customer or to a broad customer base with a non-specific message. Answer the following questions to help you come up with a highly focused buyer persona:

- Age
- Location
- Job Title
- Income
- Pain Points (that your business can solve)
- Most Used Social Network

Step 3: Create A Social Media Mission Statement

"What makes you weird, makes you unique and therefore makes you stand out." – Dan Schawbel

Your social media mission statement will drive your future actions, so make sure you put some thought into it. This statement will make it clear exactly what you plan to use your social media presence for and should clearly reflect your brand identity. Keep in mind your ideal customer when trying to create this statement.

An example mission statement might be "to use social media to educate current and potential customers' about digital marketing, with a focus upon social media marketing." Once you have this statement documented, it will make it simple for you to decide what to share and create.

If it doesn't align with your mission statement, forget about it. Businesses that post randomly without a guiding mission will fail. People follow experts, not generalists.

Step 4: Identify Key Success Metrics

"If you cannot measure it, you cannot improve it." – Lord Kelvin

How will you determine if your social media marketing efforts are successful? I am not just talking about gaining more followers, I am talking about making money for your business. Afterall, it is hard to rationalize spending time and money on something that isn't improving your bottom line.

Few metrics to consider measuring are:

- Conversion Rate
- Time Spent on Website or Social Media
- Reach
- Brand Mentions
- Sentiment
- Total Shares

Step 5: Create and Curate Engaging Content

"Content is where I expect much of the real money will be made on the Internet." – Bill Gates

Sadly, many businesses jump straight to this step. Hopefully, this book has made it clear that there are several vital steps that you must take before you start creating and curating engaging content to share on your social media channels.

Let's now discuss the fun part, posting to social media. You know who your ideal customer is and you used that information to create your social media mission statement. Armed with your mission statement it should be easy for you to begin creating and curating content. So, what exactly is considered content? Here are a few examples of content which you could create:

- Images
- Videos
- Blog Posts

- Company News
- Infographics
- eBooks
- Interviews

The list of content ideas goes on and on, but make sure you focus only on forms of content that align with your mission statement, as well as your skill set. Content is what fuels social media, so it is crucial that you consider creating high quality, engaging content as a top priority.

I strongly recommend that you create a content calendar that outlines how often you will post to each network, which topics you will share and when you will share them.

Step 6: Invest In a Social Media Management Tool

"We live in times in which ordinary people can do amazing things using the right tools"---Author unknown

Most marketers have a secret, they leverage tools to boost their productivity. Ok, maybe it isn't a secret, but without tools marketers would face constant burnout (as many do even with tools). When it comes to social media, having a social media management tool allows you to scale your efforts with ease.

One of the main benefits of a social media management tool is the ability to schedule posts ahead of time. Remember that content calendar you created? Make sure your scheduled posts in your social media management tool align with your content calendar.

Step 7: Track, Analyze, Optimize

"If you torture the data long enough, it will confess to anything." – Ronald Coase

This may be the most important step when it comes to succeeding with social media. Even the best social media marketing professionals rely on trial and error. It might seem basic, but tracking your results, analyzing the data and then making tweaks to optimize your strategy, content and tools are crucial.

Each previous step should be re-evaluated after you have had time to analyze the results of your marketing efforts. Let the data drive you. If it is telling you Facebook or Twitter is your most effective channel, consider doubling down on your time and resources within that network.

Social media marketing strategies

A great social media strategy is never set in stone, keep it flexible and change with the trends of online business and the tools that are invented. Your strategy needs to be a constant work in progress that changes with internal and external factors. So get out there, create a strategy and start optimizing it as you continue to grow and learn more about your business and your customer. Here are few social media strategies that work for everyone.

1. Integrate the efforts of your various departments

For a fully integrated social media campaign, you have to integrate the efforts of various departments like Sales, Customer service, Human Resources, Research and Development etc.

2. Focus on Networks which best suit your industry

Each network has its own advantages and disadvantages. Based on the nature and requirements of your business and target customer, you have to select the most suitable network. Given below are some of the most popular networks:

Facebook: Facebook News Feed is the best place to showcase your content. You can increase brand awareness, drive traffic and bring leads and prospects by posting your informative and inspiring content in the News Feed. Don't forget to tailor your messages to the interests of the users.

With the rapid proliferation of cell phones (especially smart phones), the percentage of Facebook users is increasing at a exorbitant rate. The growth record shows that from 40% in 2011, it rose to 60% in 2012, to 70% in 2013, to 80% in 2014 and it increases day by day.

Twitter: This is the best network for customer service and business development. You will get feedback from dissatisfied customers in real time. By responding immediately, you can rectify your business and make them happy to continue to support your business. And you can convert the happy customers into loyal customers who buy from you more frequently.

LinkedIn: It is best suited for BUSINESS TO BUSINESS social media marketers. Facebook and Twitter are more or less personal whereas LinkedIn is targeting business professionals to network their skills, create new business affiliates, do referrals of business, and to gain new employees.

Google+: The greatest advantage of Google+ is that if your presence in the site is strong, your profile will appear on top of the search engine results.

3. Inspiring and informative content

Create engaging content that will explain your business objectives with videos, infographics etc. Post your content in multiple networks like Facebook, Twitter, Google+ and LinkedIn simultaneously. Use advanced tools which help you save time and enhance your business engagement. Cover the entire social publishing process in one platform. It is good to connect to an RSS (Really Simple Syndication) feed and set up a defined schedule to auto-tweet new contents.

4. Monitoring

This is an essential part of social media strategy by which you can identify missed and potential business opportunities for your brand.

5. Engage your customers

Make sure that you are responding to customers including those who leave negative feedback on your brand and try to make them happy by rectifying the drawbacks pointed out by them. If the customers are ignored consistently, they may go for an alternative brand or business. Each unhappy customer is likely to tell nine people about their unhappiness, so your grief multiplies.

6. Track your efforts to improve your market.

Use Google Analytics and Social Media Analytics to pinpoint the messages that perform best.

7. Utilize social media as a search channel.

The latest trend shows that social media is identified as search channel for customers and can double the revenue that you receive by being a provider of searchable content. Customers goes directly to YouTube, Facebook and Pinterest for advice and opinion of the product or service before making a decision to purchase it.

Up to 80% of the customers are influenced by online reviews and comments of other customers. People are always interested in getting a friendly advice from customers with whom they can relate. Besides that, they get timely information regarding the discounts and offers which then motivate them to make an instant decision to buy it before the termination of the offer or discount.

8. Cope with the latest trends in social media marketing.

Social media marketing is not governed by the same laws of attraction and attention. New networks like Snap-chat and Periscope are ever evolving. When new media options come into play, the old ones are compelled to be more innovative by adding new features because the rules of social media are prone to change from time to time.

Conclusion

There are no shortage of strategies in social media marketing. New and innovative strategies are evolving with the development of technology. The success of your strategy will be determined by how well it is implemented, both its consistency and flexibility, which is easier said than done.

Your strategy needs expertise in techniques as well as software technical support. So, it is recommended that you seek the support and guidance of marketing agencies well-equipped with experts who can manage your social media marketing successfully resulting in an unprecedented increase in revenue.

CHAPTER 3-COMBINING SEO AND SOCIAL MEDIA MARKETING STRATEGIES

Search engine optimization (SEO) and social media-you can't do one without the other. For a business to succeed fully in its digital marketing endeavors, it must incorporate both SEO and social media marketing strategies into its overall plan.

SEO is the process of integrating keywords into content to attract more potential customers to a website or blog. It's not enough to use whatever keyword pops into your mind. Choose those which are most often used by people searching for products and services related to what you offer. Fit your marketing to your market.

One tool that can help you in finding the right keywords is Google AdWords Keyword Search Tool. When you put the right keywords in your content, it would be easier to gain a top ranking in search engines like Google. And the higher your website's rank is, the more visits you will enjoy, which will result in sales. Remember, most internet users check only the first few pages of their search results so improving your ranking to the first page should be your goal.

Social media, on the other hand, refers to networks or online communities of people and entities. It's all the rage these days. Individuals from politicians to celebrities to everyday people, and businesses from small scale companies to large corporations take advantage of it's power in spreading messages.

It's a very effective way of expanding your network of contacts. It also enables a business website to gain links which enhance connections and promote optimization. Links, as you may probably know, can help alot in SEO. The more incoming links for a certain website, the higher ranking it enjoys in the search engines.

There are countless social sites to choose from. On top of the list are Facebook, Twitter, YouTube, Pinterest, Instagram and LinkedIn. Each of these has its own features and offerings. Though it's tempting to be on every platform, it's best to choose two to three which will work most to your advantage.

How does the SEO and internet work together?

So how exactly does SEO and the internet work together?

One important SEO tactic is posting informative content on blog sites. These blog posts need to have the right keywords to get indexed by the search engine. But your work doesn't stop there. You need to promote each of your blog posts to get as many visits and clicks and comments as possible.

The easiest way to do that is by posting a link on your social accounts. If you have 2,000 fans in your Facebook page, then you can easily promote your blog article to those 2,000 people with one click. How easy and practical is that?

And every time people comment on your posts, this can further increase traffic. When a video, blog post, or website spreads like a wild-fire across social sites, that's what you call viral marketing. It's one of the things to aspire to in social media marketing.

This is just one way of looking at how SEO and social media can work together. There are many more ways that you may want to explore.

Developing and launching a digital marketing campaign should definitely involve both SEO and social media for better chances of achieving success.

Paul D. Kings

CHAPTER 4-SOCIAL NETWORK AND IMPROVING YOUR NETWORKING SKILLS

So, you have joined a bunch of popular social networks, added hundreds of friends - many of them just random people you probably don't even know - and then click the 'like' and 'share' button for every other post and tweet. Does that make you a good social networker? Do you think you have got the hang of this social media marketing craze?

Networking does not only mean that you add a bunch of friends and solicit links or comments. It is about building strong online communities and maintaining relationships for a purpose. It is the purpose that is important. Instead of just socializing, networking is done for a certain purpose. For example, to expand the number of one's business and/or social contacts by making connections through individuals.

Developing a strong social network takes time and effort, not to mention certain key skills. Whether you are an online marketer, a business person looking to boost your network, a job seeker, a teacher, or a student. Social networking skills help you get the right response and popularity in an online community of internet users. From traditional social networking sites to ones that cater to groups who have shared interests, hometowns, employers, schools, and other commonalities, here are some tips about becoming not only media savvy, but media savvier.

10 Tips to Improve Your Social Networking Skills

Determining Your Purpose in the online community.

Of course, we all know that social networks are a great way to connect with a number of people, without having to shell out a lot of money. However, finding the main purpose is important for planning your social networking properly. There has been a huge increase in the number of social media networks over the years.

Without any defined strategy and purpose, you would be wasting most of your time targeting the overwhelming number of social networks. Moreover, a proper plan is also necessary if you need to find the right customer for the message that you want to pass on through the social platform.

There is no point in wasting time trying to interest 'everybody'. Instead, work to find a relevant group or a network with people who are passionate and enthusiastic about what you have to offer. You can expand your reach from a targeted group of customers outward to their friends and family to take advantage of the peer pressure and social buzz that you can create about your brand, product or service.

Focus on Certain Social Media Networks

The number and variety of social networks available has skyrocketed in recent years. Unlike the past, where traditional networks dominated the social network scene, today, there are a number of specialized networks that are meant for people with the same passions, goals, or aims. These sites cater to a particular niche, and to improve your skills, you can pick the ones that will give you better results. Of course, you cannot ignore the biggies, like Facebook and Twitter, but when you know your target customer, find the networks that target them the best.

Know the Characteristics of Social Networks

It is also a good idea to know the ins and outs of the social network you are targeting. For example, many employers use LinkedIn as their primary professional networking site, often using People Search to view the profiles of professionals.

What they do not know is that they can use LinkedIn Skills to search for skill or expertise on the Skills & Expertise page to find professionals with that skill. Stay up-to-date on the latest features of the chosen social networks to interact properly while networking online. These networking platforms are constantly reinventing themselves and adding features to attract new users, so it is imperative that you keep yourself up to date on what they are offering as far as user platforms, app capabilities, features, support offerings, and so on.

Offer Value and Attention

Your customer's attention span on social networks is very low. It is more about trends and following peer groups than traditional networks. People want value and they want it quick. Value can be in any form. For example, on blogs, value can be through content or digital products like e-books.

Giveaways, freebies, trials, and subscriptions are some ways in which you can offer value to the people that you connect with on social networks. These gimmicks help in grabbing and retaining their attention. It is a great idea to have an interaction strategy in place. So, if comments, re-tweets, and/or replies does not get a certain desired level of feedback, you can always try modifying it for a better strategy.

Although increased social interaction is important, it is also extremely important to retain attention with the social network. If you get people to notice you and then shun them, it can create an extremely negative impression. Instead, devote some time to respond to, and even share other people's content. This creates goodwill and improves your online popularity.

Scheduling Messages

It is important to be consistent in sending out the message. People connect more when there is reliability and familiarity. Consistent messages, when passed on clearly and repeatedly, helps people connect more.

One way in which you can consistently stay in touch with your network, is by scheduling your messages. Whether you are off on a long vacation or going for a business meeting, scheduling your tweets and posts helps people stay in the know about recent events, specials, discounts or content.

Using Dashboards, Comments, and Links

Use a social media dashboard to manage your account, and send a number of emails or tweets several times an hour. So, instead of having to go to each social network site to post your messages or to see what people in your network are saying, do it all in one place. It helps you save time, keeps track of your comments, and allows you to stay in sync with your online network with ease.

In a social network, comments are valuable. It means someone has thought and paid attention enough to leave a note. Comment on posts to ensure that people/users notice your presence on the network, and you appreciate their efforts.

Links draw people to the website. You can also leave a number of links on posts, updates, and tweets, to draw them into the conversation. On Facebook, you can tag or use hyperlinks to get the best results.

Utilize Mobile Apps

With the number of people owning a smartphone increasing by the day, mobile apps have proliferated in recent years. Download dedicated mobile apps of popular social networks on your smartphone to stay connected with your social media marketing at all times, even when you are on the go.

Build a Visual Personality

When someone has a great personality, and seems genuine and interesting, it is easier to connect with that person. Whether you meet someone in person or connect with them online, it is important to let your personality shine through. Be polite, even when you disagree with someone.

Badmouthing people, even if they are competitors, achieves nothing. Phrase your arguments in a polite manner. If you want more people to connect with you on a personal level, ensure that you provide information in the sections about your bio, and use the right profile pictures and backgrounds instead of pasting random pictures of Hollywood actors.

Meet Your Online Connections

Nothing beats face-to-face communication. Unfortunately, it is not possible to meet all the people in your social network. If it is possible to reach out to your online networking connections and meet them, you should definitely try doing so. If not, then try connecting via Skype or other Voice Over Internet Protocol services.

Questions and Opinions

One way in which you can hone your social networking skills is by asking for opinions, and asking questions. Bring out your message and put it across various social networks. Post questions for your readers, and encourage them to reply and give feedback about their message in their comments.

Paul D. Kings

These simple tips can help you improve your networking skills, use social media to your best advantage, and build the ultimate social network. It is also important to keep in mind that a solid social network is not built in one day. It takes time and lots of effort, but in the end, it does pay off.

CHAPTER 5-TOP SOCIAL NETWORKING SITES

Social networking has come to a long way from just being a platform for people to meet and interact, to become one of the major tools of business in the vast expanse of the Internet. That being said, the main objective of social networking websites still remains the same - to help people stay in touch with old friends and to meet and interact with like-minded individuals in the cyberspace. What has changed, though, is the way the users are using these sites nowadays.

Social networking is no more restricted to those teenagers who are looking to make new friends in the virtual world. Today, a 40-year-old businessman uses it as a recruitment tool, while a 60-year-old gentleman uses it to stay in touch will his old pals. Right from Facebook to Nexopia, all these websites have a fan following of their own.

Top 10 Social Networking Sites

With more than a hundred websites to choose from, choosing the best social networking websites is no doubt a Herculean task. One has to take various features of these websites, including how friendly the user interface is, the networking applications it has to offer and it's security features, to determine which are the best websites for social networking.

Facebook: Undoubtedly the most popular social networking website in the world, Facebook has more than 1.87 BILLION active monthly users (as of February 2017) across the world to its credit. A user base of 'almost 2 BILLION' is quite impressive, if you take into consideration that it has been increasing seventeen percent year over year.

This mammoth figure puts Facebook at the 2nd position in the list of top websites in terms of overall users (1st being Google) and makes it the top social networking website in terms of total active users. In order to register and create a Facebook account, you need to be at least 13 years old. Once you register, you get access to the wide range of services, including messages, instant messaging, creating groups, etc that it has to offer.

Twitter: Twitter is a bit different from other social networking websites, as it is more about micro-blogging through 140 character messages known as the 'tweets'. A wide range of tools make it very easy to use twitter, and this, in turn, has added to its popularity.

The online profile of twitter users is small, and thus includes very little information, as compared to other websites, which gives it an edge when it comes to security. You also get to follow people (including all those celebrities) and keep a track of what is happening in their lives. With a monthly user base of 313 million, as of June 2016, Twitter ranks 2nd in the list of top 10 social networking websites of the world.

LinkedIn: One of the top social networking sites for business development, LinkedIn has more than 467 million users across the world (as of April 2017). More of a professional networking website, LinkedIn is popular among recruiters and job seekers alike. Simply put, it is somewhat similar to job search website which is build on a social networking platform. The best part of LinkedIn is that it allows people to develop more contacts in the same field, with the intention of spreading their business.

Google+: The latest entrant in the world of social networking, Google+ (Google Plus) is also scaling the popularity charts quite rapidly. It was launched as a successor to Google Buzz, Google's previous attempt which didn't quite make it big as it was expected to, in June 2011.

As with Buzz, this service works along with Google's web-based mail service Gmail, and allows users to share messages, photos, videos, links, etc. This also means that Google+ users can access a wide range of Google products through a common interface, and this is the biggest advantage that it has over its competitors. With a user base of 375 million as of April 2017, Google+ is fast reducing the gap between itself and other websites at the top.

MySpace: MySpace is one website which boasts of almost everything, right from personalized URLs for its users to browsing without registration. It is one of the most popular website in the United States of America. Some of the most popular activities on MySpace include MySpaceTV, MySpace forums, a wide range of applications, etc. While a user base of 15 million (as of April 2016).

Hi5: Yet another social networking website which is quite popular, especially among the youths, is Hi5. Other than staying in touch with your friends, this website also allows you to play online games, listen to music, etc. More recently, Hi5 has evolved into more of a social gaming website, with the intention of providing a platform for budding game developers.

Friendster: This social networking website allows the users to make new friends, most often based on their preferences, and interact with them. It also allows the users to share messages, videos, photos, etc. With more than a hundred million registered users to its credit, Friendster is indeed one of the most popular websites in the world.

Tagged: One of the most interesting social networking platform, Tagged allows its members to meet people online for free based on their likes and preferences. It also facilitates online gaming, and allows the members to share tags and gifts.

Travellerspoint: Quite popular among travel and tourism enthusiasts, Travellerspoint allows its users to discuss their travel experiences through forums and blogs. Basically a travel guide, this website also allows its users to upload photos and maps of various tourist destinations in the world.

Paul D. Kings

About the Author, Paul D. Kings

Paul D. Kings is a Software Engineer, Father, husband, and self-published author. He likes to write about selling and making money online. Paul has been selling on eBay and Amazon since 2007.

Visit Paul's website at http://www.pauldkings.com

Want to Read More?
Find my other books at:
http://www.pauldkings.com

Do you want to learn more about Making Money Online?
visit our website:
http://www.pauldkings.com

Subscribe to our newsletter to get free information
and free books on
making money online.

One Last Thing...

If you enjoyed this book or found it useful I'd be very grateful if you'd post a short review on Amazon. Your support really does make a difference and I read all the reviews personally so I can get your feedback and make this book even better.

Thanks again for your support!

www.ingramcontent.com/pod-product-compliance
Lightning Source LLC
Chambersburg PA
CBHW021047180526
45163CB00005B/2323